COUPLES, AWAKEN YOUR LOVE!

ROBERT CARDINAL SARAH

Couples, Awaken Your Love!

Translated by Michael J. Miller

IGNATIUS PRESS SAN FRANCISCO

Original French edition:
Couples, réveillez votre amour!
© 2020 LIFE editions, L'Institut pour la famille en Europe

Cover photo by Stefano Spaziano

Cover design by Enrique J. Aguilar

© 2021 by Ignatius Press, San Francisco
All rights reserved
ISBN 978-1-62164-482-8 (PB)
ISBN 978-1-64229-172-8 (eBook)
Library of Congress Control Number 2021931407
Printed in the United States of America ∞

CONTENTS

PART TWO
Christian Spouses Facing the Challenges of Our Era

INTRODUCTION

With the profound insight that we expect from his writings, Robert Cardinal Sarah, Prefect of the Congregation for Divine Worship and the Discipline of the Sacraments, wants to help spouses and families rediscover the sources of love and the ability to revive it. This book reprints the essentials of a retreat that he preached to couples in Lourdes in May 2019, under the sponsorship of *Marie qui guérit les couples* [the French movement "Mary who restores couples"] and of the *Accueils Louis et Zélie* [an association of family counseling centers in France and Belgium, named after Saints Louis and Zélie Martin, parents of St. Thérèse of the Child Jesus]. The heart of its message is the certainty that there is a path to renewal for everyone and that no situation is hopeless.

Although Cardinal Sarah speaks to our memory, intellect, and will, his desire is above all to get to our heart. Contemplation of the mysteries of faith that he presents to us calls us to hope. Love will have the last word.

To those who labor along the path of life, Christ comes to say that he has conquered evil. Yes, Mary heals couples and families; she takes us under her mantle and abandons no one. Let us turn to her with confidence, then. Nothing and no one can separate us from the love of Christ.

Guillaume d'Alançon
Director of the European Institute
for Family (LIFE)

For more information on the European Institute for Family, please visit the following sites:

www.life-europe.fr/life-europe-uk
www.life-editions.com/life-editions-uk
www.accueillouisetzelie.fr [in French only]
www.mariequigueritlescouples.com/welcome
[click on U.K. flag]

The European Institute for Family supervises the *Accueils Louis et Zélie* and the sessions of *Marie qui guérit les couples*.

PART ONE

The Communion of Spouses in Christ

I

Married Love: Allegory of the Chalice

Dear friends, you will not be surprised if, as Prefect of the Roman dicastery in charge of Divine Worship, I choose an analogy from the realm of the liturgy in order to speak to you about marriage and, therefore, about married love: this very pure, great, and noble love that springs from the heart of spouses is like a magnificent chalice plated with fine gold. Let me explain.

What is a chalice? You who participate in Holy Mass every Sunday know very well: a chalice is a sacred vessel that holds the Most Precious Blood of the Lord Jesus, our Redeemer, at the moment of the Consecration, when the priest pronounces the words of the Lord: "This is the chalice of my Blood, the Blood of the new and eternal covenant, which will be poured out for you and for many for the forgiveness of sins."[1] Indeed, Saint

[1] Cf. Mt 26:28.

Thomas Aquinas says in the *Summa theologiae*, "by the consecration of the bread and wine there takes place a change of the whole substance of the bread into the substance of the body of Christ our Lord and of the whole substance of the wine into the substance of his blood. This change the holy Catholic Church has fittingly and properly called transubstantiation."[2] As Archbishop Robert Le Gall of Toulouse says very well in his famous *Dictionnaire de liturgie*: "According to the liturgical norms of the Church, the chalice is made of a precious or noble material, like the paten by which it is accompanied. It must be appointed only for liturgical use. The chalice and the paten become sacred vessels through the blessing that is given to them by the priest."[3]

Allow me then to make a small liturgical digression. The "chalice" is not simply a "cup". It is not just any vessel, made of ceramic or a worthless common material. Indeed, nothing is too beautiful, too precious to receive the Blood of Christ, this Blood of the Redeemer that the God-made-man, Jesus, shed on the Cross on Good Friday for

[2] Saint Thomas Aquinas, *Summa theologiae*, III, q. 75, art. 4; *Catechism of the Catholic Church*, 2nd ed. (Washington, D.C.: United States Conference of Catholic Bishops, 2016), no. 1376.

[3] Robert Le Gall, *Dictionnaire de liturgie* (Paris: Éditions CLD, 2001).

our salvation: this same Precious Blood is what we adore during Mass after the Consecration. "You know that you were ransomed from the futile ways inherited from your fathers, not with perishable things such as silver or gold, but with the precious blood of Christ, like that of a lamb without blemish or spot",[4] Saint Peter reminds us in his First Letter. Recall also Saint John Vianney, the Curé of Ars: he lived in the most extreme destitution, and the pockets of his cassock constantly "had holes in them", as we say, meaning that he used to give everything that he received to the poor, yet at the same time the Curé of Ars did not hesitate for a moment to spend enormous sums of money when it came to renovating his church, the house of God, and also acquiring liturgical vestments and sacred vessels, because, he exclaimed, "Nothing is too beautiful for the glory of God!" Thus, it would never occur to anyone—at least I hope not—to celebrate Holy Mass with a simple glass, a goblet, or a cup, except in very special, unforeseeable circumstances. However, even in that case, a receptacle that does not comply with the liturgical norms must be used by way of exception and only once in order to manifest the faith of the priest

[4] 1 Pet 1:18–19.

and of the faithful in the Real Presence of the Blood of Christ and the veneration and adoration that this involves.

I will give you an example of this right away: It happened near the town of Saint-Lô, in June 1944: the landing had just taken place, and a Catholic chaplain of the American army knocked at the door of one of the rare houses that had remained intact. A woman opened the door for him. The priest introduced himself and expressed the desire to celebrate Holy Mass: "Unfortunately," he said with a Texas accent, "I have lost the chalice from my portable Mass kit." "Never mind," the good woman replied, "I will take from my buffet the finest crystal glass, which, just this time, will take the place of your chalice. But I promise you that at the end of this Mass, this goblet will be put into the display case of the cabinet that you see there, and no one will ever use it again for drinking." So it was that many years later you could still see the crystal glass that had contained the Precious Blood of the Lord, a glass that had a unique story that the members of that lady's family liked to tell. But let us return to our subject....

In the natural order of creation, every marriage resembles a very precious *chalice*, because God is the author of it. At the wedding feast of Cana—to

which Jesus and his Mother were invited, as you
know—the guests sang, "I will raise the cup of
salvation, and I will bless the Lord", while the
water was transformed into wine, a prefiguration of what would happen at the Last Supper on
Holy Thursday. However, here it was still only
wine, although of the best quality ... for it lacked
the redemptive act of the Cross, which the Last
Supper on Holy Thursday anticipated by making
present already this unique Mystery of Redemption, which the liturgy of the Church celebrates
in the Paschal Triduum. On Holy Thursday, the
"*cup* of blessing", therefore, becomes the "*chalice
of thanksgiving*" that Jesus offers to his apostles,
because from now on it contains his Precious
Blood, which will gush from his five wounds,
including his pierced Heart.

Well, then, just as the cup of blessing becomes
the chalice of thanksgiving, or, better, the chalice of the Eucharistic Sacrifice, so too marriage,
a natural reality created and willed by God, sym-
bolized by the cup, is raised to the dignity of a
sacrament.[5] Indeed, to continue to "spin out" our
analogy, we can say that the *cup* of married love

---

[5] See *Code of Canon Law*, can. 1055 §1; Pope Francis, Apostolic
Exhortation *Amoris laetitia* (March 19, 2016), no. 63.

is in a way covered with the fine gold of the sacrament; it becomes a *chalice*, because the love of
Christian spouses, which springs from the Heart
of Christ, has its source in the redemptive act of
Christ on Good Friday. And, to our way of thinking, superimposed immediately on the image of
Jesus crucified, which decorates the page of every
Missal before the start of the text of the Roman
Canon or of Eucharistic Prayer I, are the images,
which are just as real, of the priest who holds
up the chalice at arm's length toward the Cross
after the Consecration: for the Sacrifice of the
Cross on Good Friday and Holy Mass are *one*, just
as, at that moment when the bread and wine are
consecrated, the crucified Jesus and the priest who
acts in the very person of Christ are *one*; in other
words, the priest acts in his name and in his place
(*in persona Christi*). Which means that for Christian spouses, Holy Mass—the one in which they
participate at least every Sunday as a family—and,
therefore, Eucharistic Communion, is the source
of their married life and, therefore, of their family
life. In particular, the conjugal prayer and, therefore, the familial prayer of Christian spouses and
of their children is deeply rooted in the Eucharist
that is celebrated, received, and adored. Or else,
if you prefer this more terse expression: "There is

no married life animated by authentic Christian prayer unless we agree to offer our life in a sacrifice of Love as a fragrance pleasing to God. There is no authentic married life without the Mass, without the Holy Eucharist." This sacrament irradiates married and family life, and therefore the prayer of the spouses, the prayer of the Christian family when they gather every evening to praise the Lord, like the sun from which the daylight originates, allows us to see clearly the marvelous creation that surrounds us. And the Holy Eucharist is, at the same time, that source of living water to which we come to quench our thirst for love after the exhausting march of the week, which we have punctuated with our daily stops during the family's evening prayer.[6] But in order for the Eucharist to be truly the mystery of the Body and Blood of Christ and for it to become our true food, our Eucharistic celebrations must not turn into theater, entertainment, a folklore festival, a cultural exhibition, an amusement, or a convivial meeting of friends belonging to the same club. The Eucharist is the memorial of the Passion, crucifixion, and horrible death of Jesus on the Cross and of his Resurrection. The Eucharist is man's

[6] See the meeting of Jesus with the Samaritan woman: Jn 4:1–42.

terrifying face-to-face encounter with God, the meeting between the Thrice-Holy God and sinful man. This meeting ought to fill us with astonishment and reverential fear of God. This meeting is an encounter of faith and love. And for spouses, it must be a moment that structures their week and gives it great spiritual fruitfulness.

The Eucharist, Source of Unity of Christian Spouses

As we said a moment ago, the Most Holy Eucharist is, indeed, the source of conjugal and family life. Moreover, just as the chalice is blessed by the priest, who consecrates it to God for his liturgical usage, so too the union of a man and a woman, which is established by their free and irrevocable consent, receives a particular blessing, which has as its name: "the nuptial blessing". By this blessing, Christ, who is really the protagonist of their matrimonial union, consecrates the union of the spouses, to such a degree that only faith enables us to comprehend its irreversible and indissoluble character when we meditate on the especially firm and severe words of the Lord: "What ... God has joined together, let not man put asunder."[1]

[1] Mk 10:9.

Let us recall also that the exchange of consent acquires its full significance and enters into the divine will when the sacrament of matrimony is celebrated at the center of the Eucharistic celebration, during which the spouses receive in Holy Communion the Body and Blood of Christ: the unity of the spouses, who "become one flesh"[2] in the flesh of the Lord, is the image in this world of the unity of Christ the Bridegroom and the Church his Bride, during the celebration of the sacrament of unity par excellence: the Holy Eucharist.

In this sense, we can state that the prayer of Christian spouses, whether they are at home or traveling, is always a *Eucharistic* prayer, because it is connected with the Holy Mass during which they received Communion the previous Sunday and with the Eucharistic celebration at which they will receive Communion the following Sunday: their desire for God, which they experience in everyday married life and in their prayer, in the depths of their heart, is expressed in the cry: "*Sitio*", that is, "I thirst",[3] which is the cry of Christ crucified and, therefore, also of the

---

[2] Gen 2:23–24.
[3] See Jn 19:28.

Christian.[4] Yes, in their daily prayer, spouses, like the thirsty deer who seeks the running stream mentioned in Psalm 42,[5] long to communicate in the Blood of Christ, in other words, to receive the love of God, that ardent furnace of Charity[6] which is his very life, the divine life, and thus the gold-plated chalice of their marital union becomes the receptacle of the Precious Blood of him who alone can quench their thirst for love, truth, and eternal happiness, Jesus Christ, our Savior and the Life of our life.

---

[4] And no doubt you know that these two words are posted beneath the crucifix that adorns all the chapels of the Missionary Sisters of Charity of Saint Teresa of Calcutta.

[5] Ps 42:1.

[6] *Fornax ardens caritatis*: from the Litany of the Sacred Heart.

3

The Triptych of Marital Love:
Delight–Sacrifice–Resurrection

Let us look now at how marital life can be irradiated by the presence of Christ our Savior and, therefore, enter into the sacrificial dimension of his life, offered for the salvation of the world. Dear friends and Christian spouses here present, for this purpose it is enough to remind you of the three stages of your meeting with your spouse, which led you to be one with him or her and, therefore, to your union and your communion in marriage. These stages are similar to those of our spiritual life. Their names are: delight or amazement, sacrifice or self-offering, and resurrection.

Delight or amazement, in other words, the unmixed joy of undivided loving, is described in the Bible's love poem: the Song of Solomon, the song of the bridegroom about his bride: "If you do not know, O fairest of women.... Behold, you are beautiful."[1] All fiancés have experienced this, and to paraphrase the Book of Genesis: "God saw everything that he had made, and behold, it was very good."[2] Spouses therefore experience the goodness of God, the beauty of creation, his love, which is a matchless delight, through the persons of the man and of the woman; the woman who is created, built up from the open side of her husband, and therefore placed at his side, having the same human nature, while being different, or rather, complementary: the woman before whom the husband exclaims in an ecstasy of love: "This ... is bone of my bones and flesh of my flesh!"[3] And this love is obviously reciprocal, because, if in the order of creation the man feels that he is incomplete without the woman, then the woman for her part finds tranquility and flourishing near him who yields to her with respect and tenderness. Thus delight builds up the couple, since it is the foundation of the exclusive, faithful, and

[1] Song 1:8, 15.

[2] Gen 1:31.

[3] Gen 2:23. See the "theology of the body" developed by Pope Saint John Paul II in a series of 129 conferences given during his Wednesday catecheses on Saint Peter's Square in Rome, from September 1979 to November 1984.

irrevocable love of the spouses, and it strengthens their indissoluble unity on the basis of the joy
of their total and absolute gift of themselves, one
to the other.

It is the same in our relation with the Lord:
every evening, at family prayer, or in their "prayer
corner", the couple come to slake their thirst
with this living water that gushes from the Heart
of Jesus, the source of the sacrament of marriage;
from it they receive ineffable joys, which they
pour out into the hearts of their children, with
these words by the holy Italian spouses who were
beatified by Pope Saint John Paul II on October
21, 2001, Maria and Luigi Beltrame Quattrocchi:[4]
"God came to place upon our faithful, fruitful
human love, which is open to others, the seal of
a supernatural love so as to make us his witnesses
and his apostles", Luigi said to Maria; and Maria
answered him: "Just think that you do not have to
wait for heaven in order to feel that you are united
to me, but already now, more than ever, more
and more.... God unites, he does not break; for
God himself is Love." I could have chosen the
example of a French couple, Saints Louis and Zélie
Martin, the parents of Saint Thérèse of the Child

---

[4] Maria (1884–1965) and Luigi (1880–1951) Beltrame Quattrocchi.

Jesus: they, too, lived out this joy of the total, irrevocable gift. As you see, divorce is the biggest disaster that a husband or a wife can experience, the most irreparable misfortune and the biggest and most destructive disaster for the children.

Next comes the second stage: *sacrifice or self-offering*, which leads to the third stage, *resurrection*. Love, by its essence, involves a leap into the unknown, a death to oneself, because genuine love is a love that loves to the end. And to love to the end means to die for those whom you love. It also means to forgive them. This involves the experience, one day or another, of the Cross and, therefore, of sacrifice, which will seal the spouses' unity definitively. In other words, the definitive and irrevocable character of the marital union, which already exists objectively on the sacramental level after the exchange of consent, will become an existential reality. This is about moving on from the ecstasy of delight to the attitude of the Good Samaritan anointing with the oil of his tenderness and tact the more or less hidden wound that the spouse discovers in the soul of the one whom he loves undividedly. In other words, the disappointment that is felt one day or another when confronting a fault or a defect of the spouse, an unsuspected failing, becomes the matter for an offering of oneself in an absolute, sacrificial love, which to be sure is crucified, yet purified of all selfishness as though in the refiner's fire and in the fuller's soap.[5]

United with Jesus crucified, the Christian couple then experience a genuine "re-creation" in the order of Redemption. Indeed, the spouses can say in all truth that they are ONE on the Cross of Christ. Married life is then enriched by the dimension of forgiveness granted and received, which leads to the joy of the resurrection, in other words, to the very pure joy that can be expressed here below only in the Marian words of the Magnificat: "My soul magnifies the Lord, and my spirit rejoices in God my Savior." We can say, then, that through their sacrifice or offering of themselves to the other, the spouses leave the banquet hall of the wedding of Cana in order to taste already the ineffable joys of the eternal wedding feast of the Lamb: of Christ the Bridegroom and his Bride the Church. They do this, in other words, through the Church, which is the sacrament of salvation[6] and of all humanity, a reality of which Christian spouses are the sign through

[5] See Mal 3:2.

[6] See Vatican Council II, Dogmatic Constitution on the Church *Lumen gentium* (November 21, 1964), no. 48.

the sacrament of marriage: "Let us rejoice and exult and give [God] the glory, for the marriage of the Lamb has come, and his Bride has made herself ready."[7]

---

[7] Rev 19:7.

4

The Divine Mercy, Foundation of the Communion between the Spouses

Adam and Eve formed a family in the complementarity of man and woman. It is true that there can be no marriage, and therefore no family, apart from this otherness. This must be restated firmly and unambiguously: when society proposes to us all sorts of counterfeit marriages, which are genuine masquerades, with the slogan "Marriages for everyone", this is, to put it bluntly, an insult against the truth of marital and family life. Indeed, not all relationships are sources of life. When they cheat with reality and truth, when they attack man and woman as God willed them to be and institutionalize deviant conduct in an inconsistent and unnatural manner, one day or another this lethal phenomenon unfailingly turns against humanity with its share of violence and sufferings. Now these deviant behaviors remind us, if necessary, that love needs to be saved. The first couple, which inaugurated the history of humanity, show us in the Bible the reality of love as a source of life founded on the meaning of the otherness and complementarity of man and woman; however this is quickly destroyed by the lie introduced by Satan, the Father of lies. Since desire is no longer mastered, the couple's relationship loses its stability and security and turns into jealousy, which can lead to murder. Are we forgetting this major lesson of history and of biblical revelation?

God is love; it is not we who loved God. Rather, he first loved us.[1]

God is, therefore, at the origin of marital love, and, by that very fact, he guarantees its fidelity and, therefore, its stability and solidity. He commits himself in a promise to save wounded love by founding it on a faithful covenant with himself. The Bible's statements are realistic, because it records stories of families that are wounded and sometimes abnormal, in which sin abounds, as though to show us that salvation is offered to everyone and that God displays in this way the greatest mercy imaginable. For example, there is the sad case of the prophet Hosea, whose fundamental mystical experience

[1] See 1 Jn 4:10, 19.

enables him to discover a new aspect of God. In his troubled married life, Hosea experienced the trial of betrayed love, the wound caused by children of adultery, but he also had the strength to discover forgiveness and its purifying power. His trial allowed him to discover that love demands much humility and persevering constancy. All these personal trials taught him to look at the Lord in a new way: it is about the very experience of sin and about the love of God, which is stronger than sin and has mercy. The prophet Hosea shows us that God welcomes his Spouse Israel again and again, despite her repeated infidelities, her adulteries. God will never agree to divorce his Spouse Israel. Much later, in a beautiful allegory taken from the prophet Hosea, Ezekiel, too, in chapter 16 of his book, sets forth the whole story of the marriage between God's love and his people Israel. The latter in a cowardly way betrayed her marital promise, and for that she was chastised. However, her persistent sinfulness makes her wronged Husband's burst of kindness all the more striking. Indeed, his love for his Spouse is so immense and so strong, so faithful and so constant, that it is impossible for him to abandon her. The very power of the forgiveness, apart from any idea of merit, is therefore the most tangible chastisement that the shameful Spouse must endure. Thus God avenges himself and chastises us by forgiving us. God's vengeance is to love us and to forgive us immeasurably. And this undeserved forgiveness cannot help but arouse profound remorse for our sins, repentance, and our radical conversion. The love that God experiences for each one of us allows us to flee from sin, as one would flee from a serpent whose bite is instantly lethal. The love of God helps us to detest sin and to convert. Thus, any pastoral approach that does not aim to lead "wounded families" toward conversion, reconciliation, and the renewal of the covenant, but instead opens wide the doors to cohabitation, divorce, and remarriage, is a pastoral approach that fights against God and against the Divine Mercy. Jesus himself came to live at the heart of this tragic reality of human sinfulness. It is enough to read his genealogy cited in the Gospels of Saint Matthew and Saint Luke to be convinced of this, since we can see in it the names of persons whose lives involve problematic and immoral situations. Christ thus comes to take humanity in the midst of its sin for the salvation of all. This is what is at stake in the Divine Mercy that must pour out on our families, in which jealousy, discord, and profound rifts sometimes prevail.

5

Achieving the Communion of the Spouses in Jesus, the Redeemer

Jesus was born into an ordinary family, to a father and a mother who devoted themselves to the tasks of everyday life. He also had fraternal ties with several cousins. His family, which we call the Holy Family, serves as a model and, therefore, as a reference point for the many diverse and varied situations of all other families. On the roads of Palestine, Jesus reaffirmed God's plan in his preaching by emphasizing that man and woman are called to love one another and to commit themselves in a faithful, irrevocable, and indissoluble bond of marriage. Now some want to bring Jesus down by trying to get him to contradict Moses. The Lord does not let himself be trapped in that impasse, because he clearly affirms the primacy of the law of *love* over the law of *divorce*, which is not egalitarian. Therefore, he invites the people of God, whose understanding of marriage remained limited since the time of Moses, to take a decisive step forward. They must go beyond the teaching of Moses by returning to the divine origins of marriage, in which no one, absolutely no one, can separate what God has joined.

> Now when Jesus had finished these sayings, he went away from Galilee and entered the region of Judea beyond the Jordan; and large crowds followed him, and he healed them there.
>
> And the Pharisees came up to him and tested him by asking, "Is it lawful to divorce one's wife for any cause?" He answered, "Have you not read that he who made them from the beginning made them male and female, and said, 'For this reason a man shall leave his father and mother and be joined to his wife, and the two shall become one'? So they are no longer two but one. What therefore God has joined together, let no man put asunder." (Mt 19:1–6).

Christ thus founds married life anew on the meaning of the fidelity, stability, indissolubility, equality, dignity, and uniqueness of the love between husband and wife: it is not permitted to repudiate the other spouse for any reason whatsoever. Certainly, there is often a discrepancy between God's plan and the way in which love is experienced due to the hardening of the human heart. This gap is a source of tension and misunderstanding, but it is also a subject for reflection, for an effort at conversion so as to be able to correspond better to the abundance of the divine love and mercy.

Jesus came to save human love. He invites us to live by the love of God thanks to fidelity, peace, and forgiveness. These are the virtues of Divine Love that are realized at the heart of family life. Jesus experienced them in his family in Nazareth and also in contact with other families, like that of Martha and Mary and their brother, Lazarus, and that of the apostle Peter. He also crossed paths with the Samaritan woman, whom he invited to change her life and conduct radically, telling her that her one and only genuine marriage was the first, "for you have had five husbands, and he whom you now have is not your husband; this you said truly."[1] The teaching of Jesus is unambiguous: there is one and only one marriage, and it is indissoluble. And there is no marriage except between a man and a woman in their otherness and fruitful complementarity. He also met Zacchaeus and the widow of Naim. Confronted with various family situations, Jesus always speaks the

[1] Jn 4:16–18.

words that illuminate the life of each person, calling him to stand up and to convert to the meaning of love willed by God. Certainly, Jesus is far from being insensitive to the frailty of the feelings that distort the meaning of love, particularly the fact of adultery, of infidelity, of jealousy and lying. But he never approves sin or consents to it. When he gets to a person's heart, Jesus descends with him into the depths of the truth, he renews the person and reorients him along the lines of the evangelical demands of love, and he saves the person. Spouses, therefore, need to understand and to receive this Divine Mercy, which renews their bonds of fidelity in the sacrament of marriage.

6

Forgiveness and Mercy at the Service of the Unity of the Christian Home

The model of marital and family life renewed by the forgiveness and mercy of God is found in the parable of the Prodigal Son welcomed by his father. This son got up to return to his father and to beg his forgiveness so as to be reconciled with him in the truth and unity of their family relationship. Even before he can ask his father to grant him his forgiveness and mercy, the latter takes him in his arms and then showers him with his affection and kindnesses, while the older brother, who had remained faithful, by his vindictive attitude keeps up the family rift, rejection, jealousy, division, and the refusal to welcome and forgive.

The family, founded on the conjugal love of the spouses, which is sanctified by the sacrament of marriage, is the place of God's call for forgiveness and mercy and also the place of the call to live in truth. Why? Quite simply because the family by definition is a reality founded on the truth of relations, on the uniqueness and indissolubility of love, and on welcoming new life. Based on the teaching of the Gospel, it educates the members in humility, in the sense of forgiveness, and calls them to overcome conflicts, lies, and betrayals. The God of all mercy teaches us that our vocation is to learn to love and also to be able to love after the image and in imitation of the Most Holy Trinity. Christ, therefore, is situated at the heart of marital and family life, in other words, at the heart of the gestures and the attitudes of the husband toward his wife, and vice versa, of the father and the mother of the family toward their children—which you seek to put into practice in trust and in truth.

In his hymn to love, Saint Paul tells how our vocation as Christians is to love. Let us return to this passage:

> If I speak in the tongues of men and of angels, but have not love, I am a noisy gong or a clanging cymbal.
>
> And if I have prophetic powers, and understand all mysteries and all knowledge, and if I have all faith, so as to remove mountains, but have not love, I am nothing.

If I give away all I have, and if I deliver my body to be burned, but have not love, I gain nothing.

Love is patient and kind; love is not jealous or boastful; it is not arrogant or rude.

Love does not insist on its own way; it is not irritable or resentful;

it does not rejoice at wrong, but rejoices in the right.

Love bears all things, believes all things, hopes all things, endures all things.

Love never ends; as for prophecies, they will pass away; as for tongues, they will cease; as for knowledge, it will pass away.

For our knowledge is imperfect and our prophecy is imperfect;

but when the perfect comes, the imperfect will pass away.

When I was a child, I spoke like a child, I thought like a child, I reasoned like a child; when I became a man, I gave up childish ways.

For now we see in a mirror dimly, but then face to face. Now I know in part; then I shall understand fully, even as I have been fully understood.

So faith, hope, love abide, these three; but the greatest of these is love.

(1 Cor 13:1–13)

Saint Paul summarizes well the Christian charter of the love of God that you are called to put into practice in your everyday marital and family life. It is a matter of learning to love in the image of God. This passage expresses the desire to be loved and to love that the Creator has placed in the heart of every person by the power of the Holy Spirit.[1] However, human feelings, various attractions, and all sorts of moods sometimes take precedence over the true, authentic meaning of love. It is neither obvious nor easy to love when love is confused with the particular selfish interests of each party. Today the word "love" is often an insidious word, because everyone puts into it whatever he wants instead of being open to its genuine content. Only God can initiate us into his love because—let us say it again—by our own abilities we absolutely cannot arrive at it: love is a grace of God that is received. Indeed, it is the expression of the divine revelation and teaching of Christ. It requires a knowledge of what it truly is, an apprenticeship in order to practice it, and an effort to remain in this reality. Outside the love of God, nothing can last, and nothing is truly authentic. Only the Cross of Christ can make us understand what love is. Only the Cross of Christ makes us stable and firm in love: *Stat Crux dum volvitur orbis*: this is the magnificent motto of the Carthusian monks, which means: "Only the Cross stands firm while the world turns." Certainly, it is possible to approximate it,

[1] See Rom 5:5.

since God placed it into the human soul, but that love can very quickly be limited, perverted, and falsified without being able to unfold in its true dimensions. Yes, all that we do apart from the love of God is wasted; it is good for nothing. It does not last.

And so let us remember these evangelical demands of love that open us up to life: "Love is patient and kind; love is not jealous or boastful; it is not arrogant or rude. Love does not insist on its own way; it is not irritable or resentful; it does not rejoice at wrong, but rejoices in the right. Love bears all things, believes all things, hopes all things, endures all things."

Saint Paul tells us that love is greater than everything else and that anything accomplished in the name of God's love will not pass away; the rest will slip away like dust. This is why love is the source of the divine mercy, which must irradiate marital and familial life. Christ came to save love by dying on the Cross, so as to enable us to love and to stand up in the name of God's love and to help our neighbor up in the name of mercy.

7

The Family at the Heart
of the Church

The family is the fundamental unit and main-spring of society. It is also the foundation [*socle*] of the Church. Therefore, it is incumbent on the family in the first place to witness to Christ, who is the Way, the Truth, and the Life.[1] We have seen that the love of a man and a woman in marriage is the most sublime expression and the tangible sign of God's love for humanity in Jesus Christ. It is a matter of a covenant to which the parties must remain faithful until the end of their lives. The primary means of carrying out the New Evangelization—you know this as well as I do—is personal witness, because, as Saint Pope Paul VI used to say, our era needs witnesses more than words, however beautiful they may

[1] See Jn 14:6.

be.[2] Now, the finest witness for one of your guests whom you welcome into your home some evening is to see you pray together as a family: "Where two or three are gathered in my name, there am I in the midst of them", Jesus said (Mt 18:20). A family that prays together reveals, therefore, the presence of the risen Lord Jesus, in the midst of this world that too often is orphaned: godless and fatherless. This is why the Christian family bears the beautiful name of *domestic Church*.

Christ willed to be born and to grow up within the Holy Family of Nazareth; its life was nourished by prayer and the Word of God. The family, as a domestic Church, is a community of faith in which prayer has pride of place: prayer of praise addressed to God present in its midst;

[2] Address to the Members of the Council for the Laity (October 2, 1974) ("Lay people in the Church: a living, active, irreplaceable presence"): "Modern man listens more willingly to witnesses than to teachers, and if he does listen to teachers, it is because they are witnesses. Indeed, he is instinctively put off by anything that may appear to be a mystification, façade, or compromise. In this context, we understand the importance of a life that truly echoes the Gospel!" Apostolic Exhortation *Evangelii nuntiandi* (December 8, 1975), no. 41: "It is therefore primarily by her conduct and by her life that the Church will evangelize the world, in other words, by her living witness of fidelity to the Lord Jesus—the witness of poverty and detachment, of freedom in the face of the powers of this world, in short, the witness of sanctity."

prayer of thanksgiving for the benefits received and hoped for; prayer of petition addressed to our Father in heaven from whom we expect everything; prayer of supplication to ask for God's forgiveness and mercy; prayer of silent adoration to enter into personal, intimate communion with him. The Christian family is therefore the first school of faith, and the parents are its models and teachers. But in order to be able to teach prayer to their children, the father and the mother must be themselves a man and a woman of prayer. But true Christian prayer is sustained and nourished by the Word of God and the indispensable assistance of the Holy Spirit. Every Christian family ought to be a true temple, a genuine house of God, in which a beautiful daily liturgy is experienced in the company of the Holy Family of Jesus, Mary, and Joseph.

I conclude with these luminous and forceful words that Pope Francis addressed to families on October 16, 2016, during the Canonization Mass of seven Blesseds, two of them children of this French nation of yours, which bears the beautiful title of "Eldest Daughter of the Church": the Carmelite nun Elizabeth of the Trinity and the Christian Brother Salomon Leclercq, a martyr of the French Revolution:

Saint Paul writes to Timothy, his disciple and co-worker, and urges him to *hold fast* to what he has learned and believed (cf. 2 Tim 3:14). But Timothy could not do this by his own efforts: the "battle" of perseverance cannot be won without prayer. Not sporadic or hesitant prayer, but prayer offered as Jesus tells us in the Gospel: "Pray always, without ever losing heart" (Lk 18:1). This is the Christian way of life: remaining *steadfast* in prayer, in order to remain *steadfast* in faith and testimony. Here once again we may hear a voice within us, saying: "But Lord, how can we not grow weary? We are human ... even Moses grew weary ...!" True, each of us grows weary. Yet we are not alone; we are part of a Body! We are members of the Body of Christ, the Church, whose arms are raised day and night to heaven, thanks to the presence of the Risen Christ and his Holy Spirit. Only in the Church, and thanks to the Church's prayer, are we able to remain steadfast in faith and witness.

We have heard the promise Jesus makes in the Gospel: "God will grant justice to his chosen ones, who cry to him day and night" (cf. Lk 18:7). This is the mystery of prayer: *to keep crying out, not to lose heart, and if we should grow tired, asking help to keep our hands raised*. This is the prayer that Jesus has revealed to us and given us in the Holy Spirit. To pray is not to take refuge in an ideal world, nor to escape into a false, selfish sense of calm. On the contrary, *to pray is to struggle*, but also to let the Holy Spirit pray within us. For the Holy Spirit teaches us to pray.

He guides us in prayer and he enables us to pray as sons and daughters.

The saints are men and women who enter fully into the mystery of prayer. Men and women who *struggle with prayer*, letting the Holy Spirit pray and struggle in them. They struggle *to the very end*, with all their strength, and they triumph, but not by their own efforts: the Lord triumphs in them and with them.... Through [the] example [of the saints] and their intercession, may God also enable us to be men and women of prayer. May we cry out day and night to God, without losing heart. May we let the Holy Spirit pray in us, and may we support one another in prayer, in order to keep our arms raised, until Divine Mercy wins the victory.

PART TWO

Christian Spouses Facing
the Challenges of Our Era

I

"Your Model Is a Child"

Professor Jérôme Lejeune once said: "If someone really wants to attack the Son of man, Jesus Christ, there is only one way, and that is to attack the sons of men. Christianity is the only religion that says, 'your model is a child', the infant in Bethlehem. When they have taught you to despise the child, there will be no Christianity left in this country."

We can say that the battle of Christian spouses who want to defend the unity, indissolubility, and holiness of marriage and of the family, with truth and charity as their only weapons, is hand-to-hand combat. It is an integral part of the final battle between God and Satan mentioned in the Revelation of Saint John. Confronted with the arrogance of the Goliath of the financial and media powers that be, heavily armed and protected by the armor of their false certainties and by new anti-life laws, the Catholic Church of the twenty-first century, at least in the West, resembles little David, with his slingshot and his five stones, as Sacred Scripture tells us. Indeed, the Catholic Church, this David, has at her disposal only one slingshot—the power of the Holy Spirit—and the little pebble of the Gospel of Life and of Truth, and yet we are certain that she will strike the giant in the middle of his forehead and bring him down. In fact, as we know well, this is a very bitter and decisive battle; it will be long, and it resembles the one in the end times described in the last book of the Bible. And so what is at stake is the survival of humanity itself. The "great red dragon, with seven heads and ten horns", the prototype of this culture of death that was denounced by Saint John Paul II in his teaching, stands in front of the pregnant woman, ready to devour her child at his birth, and to devour "us", also. Its tail sweeps away a third of the stars from the sky and casts them down to earth. It is the symbol of the demonic power that dominates the world.[1] This has happened very often in the long, bi-millennial history of the Church, but let us be aware that once again the Church is the last rampart against barbarism. Today, it is not about Attila and his Huns,

[1] See Rev 12:14.

whom Saint Genevieve stopped outside of Paris in 451, or about the battle of the twentieth-century popes—from Pius XI to Saint John Paul II and Benedict XVI—against the various forms of totalitarianism that bloodied Europe and the rest of the world; this is about an antiseptic, terribly efficient barbarism in the laboratory, which public opinion hardly notices because it has been anaesthetized by the Goliaths, the financial and media powers that be. Yes, we are indeed talking about a battle ... of life and death. If this were not the case, why would the public authorities in France try to silence the pro-life websites by inventing the crime of "digital obstruction of abortion"? During the discussion of this aberrant bill in the French Parliament, the defenders of life were verbally lynched for having dared to recall that abortion is not a right, but a crime and, therefore, the greatest tragedy of our times....

2

Christian Family vs. Libertarian World:
A Head-On Conflict

Carlo Cardinal Caffarra, Archbishop Emeritus of
Bologna and the first President of the John Paul II
Institute for Studies on Marriage and Family,
stated during an interview dating back to February 16, 2008: "When I was appointed by the
Holy Father as first President of the John Paul II
Institute for Studies on Marriage and Family,
I received a letter from Sister Lucia of Fatima,
which can be found in the archives of the institute. She unambiguously told me: 'The final battle between the Lord and the kingdom of Satan
will concern marriage and the family.' However,
she added, 'Have no fear, because all who act to
promote the sanctity of marriage and the family
will always encounter opposition; some will fight
against them with every possible means, because

the stakes here are decisive. However, Our Lady has already crushed Satan's head.' "[1]

For his part, during his Apostolic Journey to Fatima, Pope Benedict XVI, in an interview on May 11, 2010, was not afraid to declare that "This too is something that we have always known, but today we are seeing it in a really terrifying way: that the greatest persecution of the Church comes not from her enemies without, but arises from sin within the Church, and that the Church thus has a deep need to relearn penance, to accept purification."[2]

Every day Christian families throughout the world are under attack. For example, gender ideology is supported, promoted, and practiced by international organizations of the UN (United Nations) and by many educational and healthcare institutions that are headquartered in the Western countries (North America, Western Europe, and Australia–New Zealand). All countries that refuse

---

[1] *Voce di Padre Pio*, March 2008.

[2] Interview with the Journalists during the Flight to Portugal (May 11, 2010), http://www.vatican.va/content/benedict-xvi/en/speeches /2010/may/documents/hf_ben-xvi_spe_20100511_portogallo-inter view.html. For the purposes of this conference, these sins that are committed in the Church are the silence, the compromises, and therefore the cowardice of a certain number of clergymen who are afraid to give witness to the truth about marriage and the family.

to adhere to this ideology are generally sanctioned or undergo strong pressure to force them to integrate it into their development program.

During his Apostolic Journey to Manila, Pope Francis did not hesitate to denounce vigorously an "ideological colonization of our families"[3] that seeks to destroy them by infiltrating and spreading through the societies and the cultures of developing nations. In no. 56 of his Apostolic Exhortation *Amoris Laetitia*, he strongly criticizes "gender ideology"

> that denies the difference and reciprocity in nature of a man and a woman and envisages a society without sexual differences, thereby eliminating the anthropological basis of the family. This ideology leads to educational programmes and legislative enactments that promote a personal identity and emotional intimacy radically separated from the biological difference between male and female.[4]

Francis Cardinal Arinze, commenting on these words of Pope Francis, said, that "the mass media

[3] Address to the World Meeting of Families in Manila (January 16, 2015), http://www.vatican.va/content/francesco/en/speeches/2015/january/documents/papa-francesco_20150116_srilanka-filippine-incontro-famiglie.html

[4] See Apostolic Post-Synodal Exhortation *Amoris laetitia* (March 19, 2016), no. 56.

are also used to banalize, secularize, and even commercialize marriage and the family."[5] This is quite evident in the programs marred by eroticism and pornography that are aimed even at children: in many Western countries, from kindergarten on, children are "reeducated", in other words, their consciences are manipulated and polluted. In some countries, the families have no choice. Thus, in 2006, in Germany, the authorities tried to force a Protestant Christian family with eight children to participate in shocking experiments in the name of sexual education. The parents decided to stop sending their children to these classes; they were sentenced to a term in prison ...

I myself, in the book *God or Nothing*,[6] vigorously denounced the frontal attacks on the family, particularly in African countries, which are being subjected to a new colonialism by the Western countries, either directly or else by way of international organizations that these states dominate and shamelessly monopolize.

---

[5] Preface, *Christ's New Homeland—Africa: Contribution to the Synod on the Family by African Pastors* (San Francisco: Ignatius Press, 2015), p. 8.

[6] Robert Cardinal Sarah, *God or Nothing*, trans. Michael J. Miller (San Francisco: Ignatius Press, 2015).

3

Spiritual Combat by Way of the Cross

Every Christian home, every couple united by the sacrament of marriage, is confronted with the challenges that we have just mentioned and is therefore called to enter into what Saint Paul calls the spiritual combat against the forces of evil that lead to death. While the apostle was traveling throughout the Mediterranean region to make Christ known, he had to confront a sizeable and unremitting adversary. Incidentally, he mentions this constant struggle in his Second Letter to the Corinthians: "And to keep me from being too elated by the abundance of revelations, a thorn was given me in the flesh, a messenger of Satan, to harass me, to keep me from being too elated. Three times I begged the Lord about this, that it should leave me, but he said to me, "My grace is sufficient for you, for my power is made perfect in weakness."[1]

[1] 2 Cor 12:7–9.

Several times in his letters, Saint Paul mentions this reality of the spiritual combat, which is inherent to all Christian life, for instance, in this famous passage from his Letter to the Ephesians: "Put on the whole armor of God, that you may be able to stand against the wiles of the devil. For we are not contending against flesh and blood, but against the principalities, against the powers, against the world rulers of this present darkness, against the spiritual hosts of wickedness in the heavenly places."[2] However, as Saint Paul himself says in his First Letter to the Corinthians, "God is faithful, and he will not let you be tempted beyond your strength, but with the temptation will also provide the way of escape, that you may be able to endure it."[3] It is true that in the life of Saint Paul—and this is the case with every baptized person—the devil did not have the final word. He says this proudly in his Second Letter to Timothy: "I have fought the good fight, I have finished the race, I have kept the faith. From now on there is laid up for me the crown of righteousness, which the Lord, the righteous judge, will award to me on that Day; and not only to me but also to all who have loved his appearing."[4]

[2] Eph 6:11–12.
[3] 1 Cor 10:13.
[4] 2 Tim 4:7–8.

We know that Christ waged the spiritual combat—that of every Christian—by offering his life on the Cross and, therefore, by sealing the New and everlasting Covenant in his Blood. On the Cross, Christ's arms were outstretched and open; his hands were nailed to the wood of the Cross,[5] the pledge of the definitive Victory through the sufferings of his redemptive Passion. As the Word of God declares through Saint Paul in the Letter to the Colossians,[6] on Good Friday, on Calvary, Christ disarmed the principalities and powers and made a spectacle of them in view of the whole world by triumphing over them through the Cross. In other words, the adversary, Satan, had his head crushed. This is why we ourselves, through our faith in the Redemption accomplished on the Cross, are delivered from all slavery of sin. We are delivered from our grudges, from our wicked thoughts, from the wounds in our past, and—the greatest victory of all—we are protected from hell. From now on, therefore, as Saint Maximus of Turin,[7] a Father of the Church,

[5] "Stretching out his hands, when his members were fastened with nails": *Confixa clavis viscera, tendens manus*. From the hymn "Vexilla Regis".

[6] Col 2:15.

[7] Saint Maximus of Turin, early fifth century A.D.

says, when a Christian prays, "he lifts up his hands to heaven, and traces a cross. If he prays with his hands uplifted, it is so that his body itself might profess the Lord's Passion." For a Christian, praying is entering into the mystery of the Passion of Christ and of his death on the Cross, and begging the Father with him for the forgiveness of the sins of mankind and obtaining eternal salvation for them.

4

The Sacrificial Dimension
of the Life of Christian Spouses

The marital life of Christian spouses has a sacrificial aspect that is rooted in the sacrament of
marriage. Obviously, the word "sacrifice" is not
at all fashionable nowadays; it is even frighten-
ing in the hedonistic context in which we live.
And yet authentic marital life—which, as we
said yesterday, necessarily has a *Eucharistic* dimension and fits into the offering of Christ on the
Cross that is made present during Holy Mass—
involves a sacrificial dimension that fits into the
spiritual combat. Even before the commitment to
protect and promote the sanctity of the marital
bond and of human life, this struggle against the
forces of evil that try to destroy the couple's unity
takes place chiefly within the framework of the
spouses' prayer, not to mention fasting and penance. Indeed, Saint Paul considers prayer to be

a kind of combat, a contest with God: "I appeal to you, brethren, through our Lord Jesus Christ and by the love of the Spirit, to strive together with me in your prayers to God on my behalf."[1] "Epaphras, who is one of yourselves, a servant of Christ Jesus, greets you, always remembering you earnestly in his prayers, that you may stand mature and fully assured in all the will of God."[2] Jacob himself wrestles with Someone (God) until sunrise and tells him: "I will not let you go, unless you bless me."[3] Prayer truly is a struggle, wrestling with God until he reveals his Name to us.

[1] Rom 15:30.
[2] Col 4:12.
[3] Gen 32:26.

5

Sacrifice, the Fruit of the Spiritual Combat

So we have come to the heart of our theme: *"sacrifice" is the fruit of the spiritual combat*, that of Moses against those who wanted to exterminate the people of God. This battle of Moses against the enemies of the people of God prefigured the definitive combat, that of Christ against Satan, the Prince of this world, who in our time is working to destroy marriage and the family by his malignant minions in the world, particularly those who write and pass unjust laws against the unity of the marital bond, against life, and especially against the life of the child in his mother's womb. This theme of spiritual combat is presented by Saint Paul as follows:

> Therefore take the whole armor of God.... Stand therefore, having fastened the belt of truth around your waist, and having put on the breastplate of

righteousness, and having shod your feet with the equipment of the gospel of peace; besides all these, taking the shield of faith, with which you can quench all the flaming darts of the Evil One. And take the helmet of salvation, and the sword of the Spirit, which is the word of God. Pray at all times in the Spirit, with all prayer and supplication. To that end keep alert with all perseverance, making supplication for all the saints, and also for me.[1]

God no longer is the one who arms himself in order to defend his people, as in Isaiah,[2] but rather it is the Christian in this world who, because he expresses his faith, is exposed to all sorts of fierce opposition. This image of the spiritual combat makes sense only in the Lord. It consists neither of steel and iron weapons that have to be carried nor of a homicidal combat that has to be waged; it is neither the establishment of the Kingdom of God by armed force nor dominion that is to be exercised in its name. Remember the reaction of Jesus in the Garden of Olives. Simon Peter, who was carrying a sword, drew it then, struck the high priest's servant, and cut off his right ear. Jesus said to Peter: "Put your sword into its sheath."[3]

[1] Eph 6:13–19.
[2] See Is 59:15–18.
[3] Jn 18:10–11.

It is a matter of putting on the power of the risen Lord, the very armor of God that, incidentally, includes more defensive than offensive weapons. This is a far cry, therefore, from the attitude of relaxation of the "Zen" or pseudo-Buddhist type, which is advocated by some therapists in order to relieve the stress of Western man who is grappling with his existential anguish.

6

The Weapon of Prayer

The Lord Jesus himself invites us to pray always and not to lose heart.[1] He gave us the perfect example for our own life. One of the predominant aspects of his life was essentially prayer—intense prayer. How many times the evangelists insistently declare and tell us: "[Jesus] went up into the hills by himself to pray."[2] "Remain here, and watch [and pray] with me."[3] "But he withdrew to the wilderness and prayed."[4] "All night he continued in prayer to God."[5] Jesus was ceaselessly absorbed in prayer. His life consisted in staying constantly in the presence of God. To pray is to remain constantly with God the Father. Not only did he give

[1] Lk 18:1.
[2] Mt 14:23.
[3] Mt 26:38.
[4] Lk 5:16.
[5] Lk 6:12.

us this example, but he also left us the very model of prayer: the "Our Father". Unfortunately, we men and women, who are superficial, materialistic, and always dissatisfied, sometimes feel that what God has given us is not enough for us. We think that it is necessary to add or subtract things. But do we really know better than God? We think that if we multiply our words, God will give us a better hearing. But we are not very concerned about our interior dispositions and the conformity of our life with the holy Will of God and about working for our Christian perfection: "You, therefore, must be perfect, as your heavenly Father is perfect."[6] "You shall be holy; for I the LORD your God am holy."[7] Like the Israelites before us, what have we done with his temple today? What have we done with the human person, with man and woman, who are created in the image and likeness of God? We profane these temples of the Holy Spirit, which are our bodies, by violating the sacred character of marriage through adultery, through infidelity, contraception, abortion, and experimentation on human embryos. We eat and drink our own condemnation by taking part in the Eucharist while in a state

[6] Mt 5:48.
[7] Lev 19:2.

of serious sin. We have turned the churches into places for a convivial meeting, into a concert hall, a museum for tourists, and have transformed our liturgies into amusements, diversions, and folklore or cultural displays, instead of respecting them as Houses, Sacred Temples of God and places of prayer. We neglect to acknowledge his Divine Presence in the tabernacle, and we have only very little reverence, respect, and deference for him. No one kneels any more before the Lord. There are even some priests who have the arrogance to mistreat the faithful by forbidding them to kneel to receive Holy Communion. Worse yet, they even go so far as to impose their lack of piety and their unheard-of irreverence toward the Divine Presence by refusing to give Communion to the faithful who get down on their knees to receive Jesus in the Eucharist. But these priests will render an account of their misuse of authority to God. Yes, we can no longer adore God in silence. No one prostrates himself any more before the majesty of the Lord, the Almighty. But with regard to prayer, the Lord also presents it to his apostles as a way of resting in the Lord, particularly when he tells them: "Come away by yourselves to a lonely place, and rest a while."[8] And so the apostles rest

[8] Mk 6:31.

with the Lord; they rest in his company and in him, listening to him and contemplating him in his ineffable mystery. It takes resolve and spiritual effort to stop all activity, even professional work, and to give up all leisure activities and even the most pressing affairs so as to give a little of your time and of your heart to God. It takes a lot of courage, faith, and love to abandon your occupations and your own interests and to offer your time to God in an attitude of listening and adoration. This is also what Saint Anselm recommends to us: "Come, take courage, poor man! Flee for a while your occupations, escape for a moment from the din of your thoughts. Cast away your heavy cares now and set aside your worries. Give a short moment to God, and rest a while in him. Enter into the chamber of your mind; banish from it everything except God or what can help you to seek him. Shut the door and start to seek him. Now speak, my heart, open up entirely, and say to God: 'I seek your face, it is your face that I seek.' "[9]

To see God, to contemplate him, to fall on our knees at his feet to adore him brings great rest and great peace to every person. However, the

[9] Saint Anselm, *Discourse on the Existence of God*.

rest I am talking about here is not the equivalent of a yoga session; it is about rest in the desert ... with God and in God. We know that, in the Bible, God often invites his people to the desert and that Jesus himself had this experience.[10] Now, is it possible to rest in the desert, that vast expanse of burning, inhospitable sand, which is inhabited only by jackals and scorpions? "Never in my life!" exclaim our contemporaries, who are accustomed to the civilization of leisure activities and incessant noise. Indeed, how can anyone rest in a deserted place, where there is no comfort, no music, no cinema, no alcohol, no expensive habits ... and the list goes on? Yes, Brothers and Sisters, the desert is not something that the frenzied, consumption-driven world seeks naturally. The fact remains that we Christians know that the true, imperishable food, the food of our souls, is not of this world. It is in heaven, and therefore it must descend from heaven to us.[11] As Benedict XVI says:

The desert is the place of silence and solitude. There you can get away from everyday activities.

[10] See the account of the temptations of Jesus, Lk 4:1–13.

[11] Compare the manna—cf. Ex 16:1–36, particularly verses 13–16—a prefiguration of the "Bread of angels" (*Panis angelorum*), with the Bread of Life—cf. Jn 6:26–71, particularly verses 48 and 58.

> There you can flee from noise and superficiality.
> The desert is the place of the Absolute, the place of
> freedom, where man finds himself confronting his
> ultimate questions. It is no accident that the desert
> is the birthplace of monotheism. In this sense, it is
> the domain of grace. Emptied of his preoccupa-
> tions, man encounters his Creator.[12]

In the solitude and silence of the desert, apart from
the world, one can finally look up to heaven and
receive fully what comes from heaven, in other
words, encounter Jesus, who is the "bread that
came down from heaven", the "Bread of Life",
and thus enter into an ever more intimate communion with him. The Lord invites us to the desert so as to give us true rest. Because—and this is
the truth—the desert without Jesus, or the false
desert of consumer goods and leisure activities, or
of the loneliness of the abandoned elderly person
and of the sick patient who waits in vain for a
visit, that desert is only an empty, sterile land that
gives rise to sadness, frustration, and depression.
On the contrary, the desert with Jesus is the gate
of heaven, where true happiness awaits us. It is the
place where we can wrestle with God the whole
night so that he will reveal his name to us.[13] So

[12] Joseph Ratzinger, *Le Ressuscité* [The risen Lord] (Paris: Desclée
de Brouwer, 1986).

[13] See Gen 32:23–32.

it was that Jacob awoke from his dream and said, "Surely, the LORD is in this place; and I did not know it." Then he added: "How awesome is this place! This is none other than the house of God, and this is the gate of heaven."[14]

---

[14] Gen 28:10–19.

7

The Good Fight for the Family

Nowadays we are witnessing in a very special way a violent, frontal combat between "the spirit of the world" and "the Holy Spirit". Let me explain. In the early days of the Church, for example in Rome, we know from Saint Paul[1] that the cultural context was rather similar to what we experience today with the trivialization of adultery, infidelity, polygamy, homosexuality, abortion.... The Christians of that era accepted no compromises but remained faithful to the Gospel, even though their witness ran counter to the prevailing culture. Thanks to the steadfastness of their example, the strength of their faith, and their unfailing attachment to Jesus Christ, they were able to be the leaven in the pagan dough of that era,[2]

[1] See Rom 1.
[2] Mt 13:33.

so that little by little they saw a conversion
of entire peoples. And so it was that Europe
became Christian and saw the flourishing of a
civilization characterized by Christianity, which
emphasized marriage, in particular the dignity of
the woman, and family, along with respect for
children from their conception. Our ancestors
in faith had therefore chosen "the Holy Spirit",
and not "the spirit of the world", although it
cost them something, namely ridicule, discrim-
ination, and even martyrdom. Now during the
two recent Synods on the Family in 2014 and
2015, in a social and cultural context very similar
to that of ancient Rome, at least in the West (dis-
dain for the human person created in the image of
God, the desacralization of sexual relations, the
human body transformed into an object of plea-
sure and commerce, the trivialization and legalization of divorce by mutual consent,[3] of temporary

[3] In France, a decision by the Court of Appeal dated December 17,
2015, ruled that adultery is no longer contrary to morality. Indeed,
in the litigation pitting Patrick Devedjian against the magazine *Point
de vue*, which the deputy accused of defamation for having revealed
an extra-marital affair, the Court of Appeal ruled that "the evolution
of morals and the development of moral ideals no longer allow us to
consider that the imputation of an act of marital infidelity would be in
itself such as to undermine personal honor or respect." Nevertheless,
despite the law dated July 11, 1975, which decriminalizes adultery,
fidelity is still enshrined in the French Civil Code (art. 212).

civil unions,[4] of contraception and abortion, of genetic manipulations and in-vitro fertilization involving the massacre of undesirable fetuses, the legalization of homosexual "marriage"[5]), the temptation to compromise with the prevailing spirit of the world today has sprung up by means of an erroneous theological-pastoral alibi: the adaptation of Church teaching to the realities of the contemporary world, or, if you prefer to put it into more theological language, the adaptation of Church doctrine to particular cases that come under the heading of pastoral care. The genuine infatuation with this model, which, however, was not a recent discovery (compare the deviant theories of Hans Küng ...), relayed by the obliging media, including Catholic outlets, won over a certain number of bishops, one of whom did not hesitate to describe this paradigm as a "fountain of revelation".

[4] Called a "civil pact of solidarity" in France, or a "pact of civil union" in Italy.

[5] Thirteen European countries (eleven of them members of the European Union) recognize homosexual marriage: the Netherlands (since 2001), Belgium (2003), Spain (2005), Sweden (2009, with a provision requiring the Church to find a pastor to celebrate religious marriages), Norway (2009), Portugal (2010), Iceland (2010), Denmark (2012), France (2013), Great Britain (England and Wales in 2013, Scotland in 2014), Finland (2014), Luxembourg, and finally Ireland (2015).

Thus the soil is now prepared for the final revolution, which corresponds also to the "final combat" mentioned by the Book of Revelation; this is the so-called "gender" revolution that turns the individual into a "zombie". This total, radical, absolute nihilism is tolling the death knell of humanity. This is the hour of combat between these shadows into which humanity sinks, held in the clutches of the demons of libertarian nihilism, and the Light that the Church alone carries like a torch, too often resembling that little flame of Hope that Charles Péguy already celebrated in verse a century ago and that no gust of wind could extinguish. For our hope in Christ, which is the foundation of our hope, in other words, our faith in the risen Jesus, the New Man, God made man, is indeed this torch that enlightens our lives and our consciences as men and women created "in the image and likeness of God".

8

The Spiritual Combat Is a Martyrdom

As Christian spouses, you are witnesses to Christ, and this is why your vocation is to resist the winds and the tides and to remain faithful to Christ and to the Gospel of Life. As you know, death *in odium fidei*, resulting from hatred of the faith, is not the exclusive privilege of that "great multitude which no man could number,... [men and women] who have come out of the great tribulation; they have washed their robes and made them white in the blood of the Lamb. Therefore are they before the throne of God, and serve him day and night within his temple", according to the vision in the Book of Revelation.[1] Such a death, in which blood is shed by Christ's witness, is not the only path to martyrdom, for it is true that a life of a Christian witness is also a life during

[1] Rev 7:9, 14.

which one offers everything to God, particularly
one's professional skills (think of all the healthcare
personnel who reject abortion, genetic manipu-
lation, euthanasia …), and also one's reputation,
and the non-negotiable human and Christian values, if they come to be trampled underfoot by the
pagans: a life in which one renounces everything
for the love of God.[2] Here is what Pope Saint
John Paul II wrote on Easter Monday, 1994, the
day after Professor Jérôme Lejeune returned to
the Father's House:

> The Resurrection of Christ stands as a great testi-
> monial to the fact that life is stronger than death.…
> Such a death [as Jérôme Lejeune's] gives an even
> stronger testimony to the life to which man is called
> in Jesus Christ. Throughout the life of our brother
> Jérôme, this call was a guiding force.… We are
> faced today with the death of a great Christian of

[2] We owe to Saint Thérèse of the Child Jesus, a Doctor of the
Church, whom Pope Saint Pius X in the early twentieth century
called "the greatest saint of modern times", this appeal to offer oneself
to God's merciful Love by way of martyrdom. Indeed, in a letter to
Father Bellière, Thérèse mentions "the martyrdom of the heart" that
is no less fruitful than "the shedding of blood" (*General Correspondence*,
Letter 213). In her Act of Oblation to Merciful Love, she exclaims:
"In order to live in one single act of perfect Love, I offer myself as a
victim of holocaust to Your merciful Love, asking You to consume
me incessantly, allowing the waves of *infinite tenderness* shut up within
You to overflow into my soul, and that thus I may become a *martyr of
Your LOVE*, O my God!"

the twentieth century, of a man for whom the defense of life became an apostolate.... We want to thank God today—him who is the Author of life—for everything that Professor Lejeune has been for us, for everything that he did to defend and to promote the dignity of human life.

9

The Holiness of Christian Spouses

"If a man loves me," Jesus says, "he will keep my word, and my Father will love him, and we will come to him and make our home with him."[1] Christian spouses are called to put into practice the teaching of the Second Vatican Council on the universal vocation to holiness[2] and, in particular, the special character of the holiness of the lay faithful.[3] Your life is, therefore, like a prolongation of the Incarnation and of the life of the Son of God here on earth. Let me explain: What is more tangible than your daily marital love with the gestures showing your sensitivity to your spouse? What is more concrete than your daily, diligent

[1] Jn 14:23.

[2] See *Lumen gentium*, ch. 5.

[3] Number 4 of the Decree on the Apostolate of the Laity *Apostolicam actuositatem* (November 18, 1965) emphasizes that "the success of the lay apostolate depends upon the laity's living union with Christ."

presence to your children and also your service to the poorest of the poor—those who are said to be "wounded by life", particularly those who suffer from the breakdown of the marital bond and of the family—with the infinite respect that you have for the laws of life inscribed by the Creator in the fibers of every human being? Christian married life makes Christ mystically present today: he heals bodies and hearts, restores sight to the blind, strengthens the limbs of the lame, enabling them to jump for joy; Jesus cleanses the lepers, opens the ears of the deaf, and loosens the tongue of the mute;[4] He who is true God and true man is also the Good Samaritan who anoints the traveler's wounds with the oil of God's love.[5] Thus we can consider your life as Christian spouses and parents, in the era of the Church in which we have been living since the Ascension and Pentecost, as a prolongation of the Incarnation of the only begotten Son of God, Jesus Christ, who came among us to heal us and save us. This is what Pope Saint John Paul II was saying in his very first encyclical, *Redemptor hominis*, when he quoted the words of the Second Vatican Council and declared that by

[4] See Mt 11:5.
[5] See Lk 10:34.

his Incarnation, Christ "in a certain way united himself with each man."[6] Concerning the marital life of Christian spouses, therefore, we can truly speak about an incarnational spirituality; together with compassion and the defense of the truth about human life, it is one of the essential features of this specific holiness of the lay faithful that makes them torches of the truth, through their example and their fight against the current degradation of our society to defend the sanctity of marriage and the sacredness of every human life ransomed by Christ.

[6] Saint John Paul II, Encyclical *Redemptor hominis* (March 4, 1979), no. 8; cf. Vatican Council II, Pastoral Constitution on the Church in the Modern World *Gaudium et spes* (December 7, 1965), no. 22.

10

The Power of Silence

Let us go further, and let us see now how your spiritual combat should be waged without succumbing to the ever-present danger of self-satisfaction or pride. In fact, when we are entirely involved in activity, we run the risk of succumbing to the following temptation, which is well known by the ardent missionaries of the Gospel: that our person, our "ego", establishes its own supremacy absolutely, surreptitiously setting God aside. I think that we can avoid that stumbling block, no doubt by means of a spiritual combat that is sometimes quite fierce. We can start by praying the Rosary; Our Lady insistently recommends that we meditate on its mysteries, here at Lourdes and in other sites of her apparitions, like Fatima, La Salette, Pontmain, Pellevoisin, Beauraing, and Banneux. Yes, we are pilgrims and witnesses of the Gospel of Life through praying the Rosary:

let Mary's words at the Annunciation resound constantly in our hearts as faithful, humble servants of the Gospel and of the Church: *Fiat!* Yes, *fiat* is the word—what am I saying?—the pure, perfect, unreserved *response* of the Most Blessed Virgin Mary, which you are called to say to God every day of your life. Hence, like the Most Blessed Virgin Mary, and also like so many saintly men and women whose response, as we know, was marked with filial abandonment (for example, Saint Thérèse of Lisieux, Saint Joan of Arc, or Saint Charles de Foucauld), we allow God to act in our whole life. "To let God" or "to consent" in Catholic spiritual theology is to agree to this union of freedom and grace that raises a human being to the rank of God's collaborator. Indeed, for a baptized person, the decision to hand control of his life over to Christ is a fundamental act that allows him to avoid the traps of ostentation, discouragement, and sadness. However, in order to do that, it is necessary to be steeped in what I will call humble "discretion", buried in God, in other words, in the *silence* that is the privilege of the great contemplatives and the true worshippers of God. And this silence is not only a royal portico by which the Most Holy Trinity enters into our soul and comes to make their home in us,[1] so as to transfigure our everyday tasks into acts of love. Silence is also a "power"; hence the title of the book that I wrote, with God's help, in 2016: *The Power of Silence*.

The world dominated by the diabolical forces of the culture of death is fighting against you today, and it will fight more and more; it will try to reduce you to silence, but far from crushing you, your *silence*, experienced in the prayer of praise offered together with the Virgin Mary in the humble meditation of our daily Rosary, will paradoxically become a veritable "power", through your closeness with God, the power of witness, of martyrdom, the power of holiness. For this silence will be the silence of Jesus during his own Passion when he faced his accusers. Based on the Gospels, let us see what the attitude of the Lord Jesus was. First of all, Saint Matthew tells us that Jesus appeared before the high priests and the entire High Council, who were looking for false testimony so as to condemn him to death. Now the evangelist says:

> But they found none, though many false witnesses came forward. At last two came forward and said, "This fellow said, 'I am able to destroy the temple of God, and to build it in three days.'" And

[1] See Jn 14:23.

the high priest stood up and said, "Have you no answer to make? What is it that these men testify against you?"

Jesus autem tacebat, the Gospel continues.

> But Jesus was silent. And the high priest said to him, "I adjure you by the living God, tell us if you are the Christ, the Son of God." Jesus said to him, "You have said so. But I tell you, hereafter you will see the Son of man seated at the right hand of Power, and coming on the clouds of heaven." Then the high priest tore his robes, and said, "He has uttered blasphemy. Why do we still need witnesses? You have now heard his blasphemy. What is your judgment?" They answered, "He deserves death."[2]

Then, according to the evangelist Saint Luke, Jesus appeared before Herod, who interrogated him at length, but he made no answer. Finally, Herod treated him with contempt, clothed him in a bright garment, and sent him to Pilate.[3] Saint John then tells us that the procurator in turn questioned him about his identity, and Jesus declared: "For this I was born, and for this I have come into the world, to bear witness to the truth."[4] Then he fell silent. He responded by ... his silence.

[2] Mt 26:59–66.
[3] See Lk 23:8–11.
[4] Jn 18:37.

As I write in *The Power of Silence*, in today's world we know that "the man who speaks is celebrated, and the silent man is a poor beggar in whose presence there is no need even to raise one's eyes."[5] Jesus had become the beggar of God's love for this sinful, deaf, and blind humanity. Let us not hesitate to meditate on the Lord's cry on the glorious Cross: "I thirst." In *The Power of Silence*, I go so far as to state that "at the most crucial moment in his life, when there was screaming on all sides, covering him with all sorts of lies and calumnies, when the high priest asked him: 'Have you no answer to make?' Jesus preferred silence."[6] Thus "Jesus, in being silent, intends to show his contempt for the lies, for he is the truth, the light, and the only way that leads to Life. His cause does not need to be defended. We do not defend the truth and the light: their splendor is their own defense."[7] For his part, Pilate "does not understand the cause of such an extraordinary silence. He is confronted with God's silence, in the midst of the howling of men who are drunk with irrational hatred!"[8] Yes,

---

[5] Robert Cardinal Sarah, *The Power of Silence*, trans. Michael J. Miller (San Francisco: Ignatius Press, 2017), no. 30, p. 38.

[6] Ibid., no. 141, p. 80.

[7] Ibid., no. 197, pp. 101–2.

[8] Ibid., no. 197, p. 102.

dear friends, Christian spouses, what could you say in response to this verbal abuse that we hear so often, even on the lips of political leaders: "A woman who has an abortion is not interrupting a life", and also: "Abortion is a woman's right"? Faced with this crudeness and this blindness, only silence can incite us to enter into ourselves and to confront the truth.

At this stage of our meditation, allow me to make this analogy: when our Christian brothers in the Middle East, who right now are suffering persecution, are arrested and imprisoned and tortured by their executioners, they can show them the cross engraved in their flesh, which is the profession of their faith as baptized Christians in case, they say, "under torture we might succumb to the temptation to deny Christ." Indeed, while so many of our contemporaries here in the decadent West, following a passing and expensive fashion, indulge in the strange practice of tattooing, those Christians are always ready to show to the Caiaphases and Pilates of our time the *Cross* that is tattooed indelibly on their own wrists, a silent witness to their union with Jesus until death. "At least", they say, "this sign will overcome my possible weakness when confronting the fear of dying." It is the same with you, Christian spouses:

your cross tattooed on the wrist is your calm statement that, as Professor Jérôme Lejeune said, "the dignity of a civilization is measured by the respect that it has for the weakest of its members." Martyrs for life and for truth, this is therefore your vocation in this world that ignores God and has banished him from its sight, and in certain hours your silence, far from being an admission of weakness, will be a *power* capable of overturning the mountains of practical atheism and indifference. As I write in *The Power of Silence*,

> Today, the silences of the Christian martyrs who will be massacred by the enemies of Christ imitate and prolong those of the Son of God. The martyrs of the first centuries, like those of our sad time, all show the same silent dignity. Silence then becomes their only speech, their only testimony, their last testament. The blood of martyrs is a seed, a cry, and a silent prayer that rises up to God.[9]

[9] Ibid., no. 198, p. 103.

II

Pro-Life Commitment

Dear friends, today no one can be insensitive and indifferent to the urgent obligation to defend the preborn child. Besides the moral aspect that forbids us to attack any human life, especially that of an innocent, defenseless person, the protection of the embryo is the *sine qua non* condition for combating the civilization of barbarism and ensuring the future of our humanity. The most impressive clinical symptom indicating that we are headed for the edge of the cliff and a bottomless pit is the dramatic increase in the rejection of life. In this consumer society, man is becoming increasingly insensitive to the sacred respect for human life. He no longer understands how the human person could be an absolute that we do not have the right to manipulate as we please.

I encourage you to follow the inviolable line of the Church: the defense of the dignity of the

human person. As you know, the public authorities themselves acknowledge as a disastrous victory the fact that 96 percent of children with
Down syndrome are put to death by abortion.
This is truly horrible, criminal, and sacrilegious!
Oppose homosexual "marriage", which is false
and scandalous, and the aberrations of surrogate
motherhood and medically assisted procreation
[for instance, in-vitro fertilization]. Energeti-
cally combat the frenzied, lethal ideas of so-called
"gender" theory. Not to mention transhumanism, which is utterly terrifying: how far are they
going to go on this hell-bent course? Indeed,
with transhumanism, this means that "augmented
humanity" will be the triumph of eugenics and
the selection of the best genetic capital from
among all beings so as to create the ideal super-
man. Thanks to technology and science, transhumanism will make the Promethean dream of
Nazism a reality. Will there be a master race, as
in Nazism? If so, by what criteria? And, in that
case, what will they do with the "subhumans",
according to the Nazi terminology, whose work
will have been replaced by robots? These questions are terrifying and blood-chilling.

The refusal to welcome those who are bother-
some and to let them live—in other words, not

only the "unwanted" child who has been con-
ceived (the constant drumbeat of abortion advo-
cates), but also the handicapped person, the patient
with a terminal illness, the elderly person who has
become helpless—this refusal shows a profound
misunderstanding of the value of every human
life created and willed by God. In the encyclical *Evangelium vitae*, Pope Saint John Paul II declares that

> we are confronted by an even larger reality, which
> can be described as a veritable structure of sin. This
> reality is characterized by the emergence of a cul-
> ture which denies solidarity and in many cases takes
> the form of a veritable "culture of death".... A
> person who, because of illness, handicap or, more
> simply, just by existing, compromises the well-
> being or life-style of those who are more favoured
> tends to be looked upon as an enemy to be resisted
> or eliminated. In this way a kind of "conspiracy
> against life" is unleashed.[1]

And Pope Francis, with the candor that we have
come to expect from him, unflinchingly describes
this "throw-away culture". "Unfortunately, what
is thrown away is not only food and dispensable
objects, but often human beings themselves, who

---

[1] Saint John Paul II, Encyclical Letter *Evangelium vitae* (March 25,
1995), no. 12.

are discarded as 'unnecessary'." And he adds: "It is frightful even to think there are children, victims of abortion, who will never see the light of day."[2] The Holy Father explains in his apostolic exhortation *Evangelii gaudium* ("The Joy of the Gospel") dated November 24, 2013:

> Among the vulnerable for whom the Church wishes to care with particular love and concern are unborn children, the most defenceless and innocent among us. Nowadays efforts are made to deny them their human dignity and to do with them whatever one pleases, taking their lives and passing laws preventing anyone from standing in the way of this. Frequently, as a way of ridiculing the Church's effort to defend their lives, attempts are made to present her position as ideological, obscurantist and conservative. Yet this defence of unborn life is closely linked to the defence of each and every other human right. It involves the conviction that a human being is always sacred and inviolable, in any situation and at every stage of development.[3]

Thus, Pope Francis call us to a general pro-life mobilization: when he mentions the Church, which, he says, is like a "field hospital" after a

[2] Pope Francis, Address to Members of the Diplomatic Corps Accredited to the Holy See (January 13, 2014).

[3] Pope Francis, Apostolic Exhortation *Evangelii gaudium* (November 24, 2013), no. 213.

battle, he is thinking in the first place about this battle for the survival of humanity, which has been terribly wounded in both body and soul, while Holy Mother Church stands at the bedside. Christian spouses are called to pour the oil of mercy and the wine of the truth that sets us free[4] onto the wounds of this defenseless part of humanity that is ignored by the powerful of this world, in this "hospital", this *Hôtel-Dieu* [hospital for the poor in Paris, founded in the seventh century], which is also the "inn" of the parable of the Good Samaritan; and we know that the inn here is the allegory for the Church, our Mother.

I take this opportunity to thank all the men and women among you who work patiently, against adverse winds and tides, for the promotion and protection of human life, as well as the family, which is its sanctuary. Life is a gift from God, a gift that God entrusted to the family. In the family, therefore, life finds its source, the setting in which it flourishes and grows, the framework that corresponds to its dignity and its destiny.

---

[4] The oil of mercy and the wine of truth: see Lk 10:34. "Jesus then said to the Jews who had believed in him, 'If you continue in my word, you are truly my disciples, and you will know the truth, and *the truth will make you free*' " (Jn 8:31–32).

Hence the sacred character of human life and the respect that it deserves—two imperatives that all legislation worthy of the name should acknowledge and promote, including here, in France, the Eldest Daughter of the Church. Indeed, in the life of each human person, even the weakest and most wounded, the image of God shines and is manifested in all its fullness with the coming and the Incarnation of Jesus, the Son of God-who-saves. Hence every person is called to a fullness of life that goes well beyond the dimensions of his existence on earth, since it is participation in the very life of God.

The Future of Humanity Passes through the Family

By way of a conclusion, I would like to quote this excerpt from the *Letter to Families* by Pope Saint John Paul II, dated February 2, 1994.[1] You will see that it has not aged in the least.

> May Christ, who is the same "yesterday and today and for ever" (Heb 13:8), be with us as we bow the knee before the Father, from whom all fatherhood and motherhood and every human family is named (cf. Eph 3:14–15). In the words of the prayer to the Father which Christ himself taught us, may he once again offer testimony of that love with which he loved us "to the end" (Jn 13:1)!
>
> I speak with the power of his truth to all people of our day, so that they will come to appreciate the grandeur of the goods of marriage, family and

---

[1] http://www.vatican.va/content/john-paul-ii/en/letters/1994 /documents/ hf_jp-ii_let_02021994_families.html

life; so that they will come to appreciate the great danger which follows when these realities are not respected, or when the supreme values which lie at the foundation of the family and of human dignity are disregarded.

May the Lord Jesus repeat these truths to us *with the power and the wisdom of the Cross*, so that humanity will not yield to the temptation of the "father of lies" (Jn 8:44), who constantly seeks to draw people to broad and easy ways, ways apparently smooth and pleasant, but in reality full of snares and dangers. May we always be enabled to follow the One who is "the way, and the truth, and the life" (Jn 14:6).

Saint John Paul II said repeatedly that "the future of humanity passes through the family." Yes, if the final battle between God and the kingdom of Satan concerns marriage and the family, it is urgent for us to realize that we are already in the center of this spiritual battle, on which the future of our human societies depends, and we know that the family, founded on loving, monogamous, free, faithful, and indissoluble marriage, is the basic cell of society. Our Christian families are like the multiple cells made of wax, fragile and always in need of reinforcement, that make up the hive, where everyone is called to taste the honey of Truth, that is to say, the saving

Words of the Lord Jesus and of his Bride, Holy Church. In this Marian city of Lourdes, may we be able to find refuge—like Mary, the Mother of the Redeemer and our Mother—in the Heart of Jesus, in his Sacred Heart that was pierced by his love for us ... before it is too late.

APPENDIX I

Conjugal Prayer

INTRODUCTION

When spouses pray together each day, their love is an impregnable stronghold. Affirming this is a good thing, but it is not always that easy to know how to pray and especially what "to say".

To help those who wish to make conjugal prayer one of the high points of their day, this booklet [*sic*; appendix] presents the essential elements in the unique encounter of the two spouses with God. The proposed plan can be adapted (by choosing other texts) while making sure to keep the structure, so as not to miss certain steps. If one of the spouses is absent, this time of conjugal "recharging" can be experienced while they are miles apart.

This prayer is composed of an act of abandonment to the Divine Mercy, a time of thanksgiving, a reading from the Word of God, and finally an original meditation for each day dedicated to a topic that speaks to the spouses (inspired by the four pillars of marriage) ... all under the watchful eyes of the Blessed Virgin, the protectress of the home.

It is not wrong to say that spouses who have put conjugal prayer at the heart of their lives have experienced an incredible renewal of their lives, bordering on the miraculous for some couples. Be careful, though; in order to bear fruit, prayer must not be irregular, one day this way, one month that way.... It is supposed to enter into everyday life as a communal meeting for two, in the sight of God.

A few minutes in return for an eternity of love.

SEQUENCE OF DAILY PRAYER

1. Make the sign of the cross, *slowly, followed by a minute of silence.*

2. Beg for Divine Mercy *while making a profound bow*:

   > My God, here we are before you with all our limitations, our sins, our wounds.... (*Make a brief examination of conscience in silence.*) We can do nothing without you, without your infinite mercy, and we humbly ask your forgiveness. We desire with all our strength, with the help of your grace, to follow the path of the Gospel. Have mercy on us, my God.

3. Conjugal chapter[1] (*to be recited by each spouse in turn*):

   > N. (*say the spouse's first name*), I ask you to forgive me for the times when I have been

---

[1] A chapter is, among other things, the time in a religious community dedicated to reconciliation among its members. This term highlights the eminent value of the Christian home as a cell of the Church that is called to live out forgiveness.

inconsiderate and may have hurt you. (*Mention one if appropriate.*)

I ask God to help me to love you more. Blessed be God for your good qualities. (*Mention one if appropriate.*)

4. Read from the Word of God, *slowly, followed by a short time of silence to let it sink in.*

5. Recite one Our Father, one Hail Mary, and one Glory Be.

6. Read the meditation for the day.

7. Prayer for Spouses:

> O Mary, we turn to you. Guide us according to God's will.
>
> Grant that we may be spouses and parents according to the Heart of your Son.
>
> Make us more united every day.
>
> Give us an ever more loving heart for our spouse, our children, and our neighbor.
>
> Keep us faithful to the Word of God.
>
> Renew in us the gifts of the Holy Spirit.
>
> May we have a heart that is poor in spirit that will guide us to God alone.
>
> O Mary, protect us from all evil, especially at the hour of our death. Amen.

SUNDAY

1. Make the sign of the cross, *slowly, followed by a minute of silence.*
2. Beg for Divine Mercy *while making a profound bow*:

   > My God, here we are before you with all our limitations, our sins, our wounds.... (*Make a brief examination of conscience in silence.*) We can do nothing without you, without your infinite mercy, and we humbly ask your forgiveness. We desire with all our strength, with the help of your grace, to follow the path of the Gospel. Have mercy on us, my God.

3. Conjugal chapter (*to be recited by each spouse in turn*):

   > N. (*say the spouse's first name*), I ask you to forgive me for the times when I have been inconsiderate and may have hurt you. (*Mention one if appropriate.*)
   >
   > I ask God to help me to love you more. Blessed be God for your good qualities. (*Mention one if appropriate.*)

4. Read from the Word of God, *slowly, followed by a short time of silence*:

> Tobias got up from the bed and said [to Sarah], "Sister, get up, and let us pray and implore our Lord that he grant us mercy and safety." And they began to say, "Blessed are you, O God of our fathers, and blessed be your holy and glorious name for ever. Let the heavens and all your creatures bless you. You made Adam and gave him Eve his wife as a helper and support. From them the race of mankind has sprung. You said, 'It is not good that the man should be alone; let us make a helper for him like himself.' And now, O Lord, I am not taking this sister of mine because of lust, but with sincerity. Grant that I may find mercy and may grow old together with her." And they both said, "Amen, amen." Then they both went to sleep for the night. (Tob 8:4–8)

5. Recite one Our Father, one Hail Mary, and one Glory Be.

6. Meditation:

> Mary, on this day when the Church celebrates the Paschal Mystery of your Son, we are in festive garments, as on the blessed day of our marriage. Today again, in every

corner of the world, Jesus makes himself present when the priest at the altar pronounces the words of consecration over the bread and the wine, which then become his Body and Blood.

If our everyday routine becomes burdensome, if educating the children, family worries, professional problems, and marital misunderstandings upset us, be with us, O Mary, to help us offer them to the Father through Jesus. Our life will thus recover its fruitfulness, and the difficulties will turn into blessings. With Jesus, who was crucified so that the world might have life, we accept trials as so many occasions to make progress in marital love and the unselfish gift of ourselves.

Most Blessed Virgin, make our life a continual Mass, an offering of love to the Father in union with Jesus. For that we need the Eucharist. And so, we ask you, give us a thirst for the Mass so as to enliven our marriage, not only on Sunday, but also during the week.

Our Lady, Mother of Jesus in the Host, pray for us.

7. Prayer for Spouses: see p. 104.

MONDAY

1. Make the sign of the cross, *slowly, followed by a minute of silence.*

2. Beg for Divine Mercy *while making a profound bow*:

   > My God, here we are before you with all our limitations, our sins, our wounds.... (*Make a brief examination of conscience in silence.*) We can do nothing without you, without your infinite mercy, and we humbly ask your forgiveness. We desire with all our strength, with the help of your grace, to follow the path of the Gospel. Have mercy on us, my God.

3. Conjugal chapter (*to be recited by each spouse in turn*):

   > N. (*say the spouse's first name*), I ask you to forgive me for the times when I have been inconsiderate and may have hurt you. (*Mention one if appropriate.*)
   >
   > I ask God to help me to love you more. Blessed be God for your good qualities. (*Mention one if appropriate.*)

4. Read from the Word of God, *slowly, followed by a short time of silence*:

The voice of my beloved! Behold, he comes, leaping upon the mountains, bounding over the hills. My beloved is like a gazelle, or a young stag. Behold, there he stands behind our wall, gazing in at the windows, looking through the lattice. My beloved speaks and says to me: "Arise, my love, my dove, my fair one, and come away; for behold, the winter is past, the rain is over and gone. The flowers appear on the earth, the time of pruning has come, and the voice of the turtledove is heard in our land. The fig tree puts forth its figs, and the vines are in blossom; they give forth fragrance. Arise, my love, my fair one, and come away. O my dove, in the clefts of the rock, in the covert of the cliff, let me see your face, let me hear your voice, for your voice is sweet, and your face is comely." ... My beloved is mine and I am his, he pastures his flock among the lilies. (Song 2:8–16)

5. Recite one Our Father, one Hail Mary, and one Glory Be.

6. Meditation:

O Mary, as this week begins, we come to entrust to you our works, those who work with us, and those who benefit from our efforts.

In Nazareth you did so much, in silence, as was your custom. Teach us the art of being calm in our activity and discreet, in imitation of Saint Joseph. As our motto, we want to "do good", and we wish to write this in golden letters on our heart.

Let everything work together to strengthen our union by the bond of the interior life: "So they are no longer two but one [flesh]. What therefore God has joined together, let no man put asunder" (Mt 19:6). We dare to say yes again to each other, to renew the exchange of our consents, and to refresh ourselves in this spring of living water that is the grace of the sacrament of our marriage.

O Mary, we entrust to you our deep unity. Grant that we may root it more and more in the mystery of love that unites Christ to his Church.

Our Lady, Mother of marital unity, pray for us.

7. Prayer for Spouses: see p. 104.

TUESDAY

1. Make the sign of the cross, *slowly, followed by a minute of silence.*

2. Beg for Divine Mercy *while making a profound bow:*

> My God, here we are before you with all our limitations, our sins, our wounds.... (*Make a brief examination of conscience in silence.*) We can do nothing without you, without your infinite mercy, and we humbly ask your forgiveness. We desire with all our strength, with the help of your grace, to follow the path of the Gospel. Have mercy on us, my God.

3. Conjugal chapter (*to be recited by each spouse in turn*):

> N. (*say the spouse's first name*), I ask you to forgive me for the times when I have been inconsiderate and may have hurt you. (*Mention one if appropriate.*)
>
> I ask God to help me to love you more. Blessed be God for your good qualities. (*Mention one if appropriate.*)

4. Read from the Word of God, *slowly, followed by a short time of silence*:

> Blessed is every one who fears the LORD, who walks in his ways! You shall eat the fruit of the labor of your hands; you shall be happy, and it shall be well with you. Your wife will be like a fruitful vine within your house; your children will be like olive shoots around your table. Behold, thus shall the man be blessed who fears the LORD. The LORD bless you from Zion! May you see the prosperity of Jerusalem all the days of your life! May you see your children's children! Peace be upon Israel! (Ps 128)

5. Recite one Our Father, one Hail Mary, and one Glory Be.

6. Meditation:

> O Mary, we are very frail but rely on your patience as an experienced mother. When the temptation to self-centeredness and egotism catches us by surprise, grant that we may be generous.
>
> We entrust our fertility to you, O Mary. We declare to you our desire to be open to new life, as responsible parents who trust in Providence. Our fertility belongs to you, whatever may happen. Grant us the goodness

that is capable of tenderness and can transform our hearts of stone into hearts of flesh.

Teach us to renew our strength often through the sacrament of penance and reconciliation, so as to live as disciples of mercy.

Yes, we believe; yes, we want to evangelize; yes, we want the Kingdom of Christ to extend on earth as it does in heaven, starting with our home. And so we entrust to you especially our children and those who are dear to us, so that they may always be faithful to Christ and his Church.

Most Blessed Virgin, you appeared so many times to people to tell them to convert and to open their hearts; grant that our country may experience a profound Christian renewal. Make us fervent missionaries of the Gospel, in our workplaces and in our free time, in our commitment to the poor, in the service of the common good....

Our Lady of Pentecost, Queen of love and Protectress of all human life from conception to natural death, pray for us.

7. Prayer for Spouses: see p. 104.

WEDNESDAY

1. Make the sign of the cross, *slowly, followed by a minute of silence.*

2. Beg for Divine Mercy *while making a profound bow*:

   My God, here we are before you with all our limitations, our sins, our wounds.... (*Make a brief examination of conscience in silence.*) We can do nothing without you, without your infinite mercy, and we humbly ask your forgiveness. We desire with all our strength, with the help of your grace, to follow the path of the Gospel. Have mercy on us, my God.

3. Conjugal chapter (*to be recited by each spouse in turn*):

   N. (*say the spouse's first name*), I ask you to forgive me for the times when I have been inconsiderate and may have hurt you. (*Mention one if appropriate.*)

   I ask God to help me to love you more. Blessed be God for your good qualities. (*Mention one if appropriate.*)

4. Reading from the Word of God, *slowly, followed by a short time of silence*:

> If I speak in the tongues of men and of angels, but have not love, I am a noisy gong or a clanging cymbal. And if I have prophetic powers, and understand all mysteries and all knowledge, and if I have all faith, so as to remove mountains, but have not love, I am nothing. If I give away all I have, and if I deliver my body to be burned, but have not love, I gain nothing.
>
> Love is patient and kind; love is not jealous or boastful; it is not arrogant or rude. Love does not insist on its own way; it is not irritable or resentful; it does not rejoice at wrong, but rejoices in the right. Love bears all things, believes all things, hopes all things, endures all things. Love never ends. (1 Cor 13:1–8)

5. Recite one Our Father, one Hail Mary and one Glory Be.

6. Meditation:

> O Mary, some hours are longer and more fatiguing than others, and we do not feel like following the daily routine. When weariness arrives in our work and our marital relationship, we ask you to keep both of us

in the sanctuary of our love and the duties of our state.

At the foot of the Cross, you endured to the end; give us the grace of perseverance. For that purpose, help us to be able to set aside days on which both of us can rest, with each other, for a time of marital renewal and spiritual retreat.

O Mary, you love each one of your children in a unique way; we entrust our spiritual growth to you. Help us to accommodate one another in our different rhythms and personal histories and in anything that could cause a conflict. Make it an occasion to build up our marital complementarity and an opportunity for personal conversion.

Watch over our fidelity: may our friendship as spouses develop, and may no disorderly passion stifle it.

Our Lady of Fidelity, pray for us.

7. Prayer for Spouses: see p. 104.

THURSDAY

1. Make the sign of the cross, *slowly, followed by a minute of silence.*

2. Beg for Divine Mercy *while making a profound bow*:

   My God, here we are before you with all our limitations, our sins, our wounds.... (*Make a brief examination of conscience in silence.*) We can do nothing without you, without your infinite mercy, and we humbly ask your forgiveness. We desire with all our strength, with the help of your grace, to follow the path of the Gospel. Have mercy on us, my God.

3. Conjugal chapter (*to be recited by each spouse in turn*):

   N. (*say the spouse's first name*), I ask you to forgive me for the times when I have been inconsiderate and may have hurt you. (*Mention one if appropriate.*)

   I ask God to help me to love you more. Blessed be God for your good qualities. (*Mention one if appropriate.*)

4. Read from the Word of God, *slowly, followed by a short time of silence*:

> When Jesus had spoken these words, he lifted up his eyes to heaven and said, "Father, the hour has come; glorify your Son that the Son may glorify you, since you have given him power over all flesh, to give eternal life to all whom you have given him. And this is eternal life, that they know you the only true God, and Jesus Christ whom you have sent.... I have given them your word; and the world has hated them because they are not of the world, even as I am not of the world. I do not pray that you should take them out of the world, but that you should keep them from the evil one. They are not of the world, even as I am not of the world. Sanctify them in the truth; your word is truth. As you sent me into the world, so I have sent them into the world. And for their sake I consecrate myself, that they also may be consecrated in truth.
>
> "I do not pray for these only, but also for those who believe in me through their word, that they may all be one; even as you, Father, are in me, and I in you, that they also may be in us, so that the world may believe that

you have sent me. The glory which you have given me I have given to them, that they may be one even as we are one, I in them and you in me, that they may become perfectly one, so that the world may know that you have sent me and have loved them even as you have loved me." (Jn 17:1–3, 14–23)

5. Recite one Our Father, one Hail Mary, and one Glory Be.

6. Meditation:

Mary, here we are, both of us, humbly at your feet. Even though we have hidden sorrows, we know that they will not be fruitless if we accept them as opportunities for growth.

We come to offer to you our freedom so as to discover its true meaning. Freely we chose each other, and freely we hand over to you all that we are.

We want to love one another in a total gift, with no reservations and no going back, because love demands this gift. Just when we might think that we are losing our freedom, in reality we find it.

To you we entrust our intimacy; may it shine with affection, respect, and nobility; may it be open to life, beautiful, and pure.

O Mary, we want to love one another and to give ourselves to each other as Jesus did: "I lay down my life, that I may take it again. No one takes it from me, but I lay it down of my own accord" (Jn 10:17–18). We want to learn from you to live each day the miracle of the gift that springs from the mystery of love that unites the Father to the Son through the Holy Spirit.

With you we want to say yes to the joy of being free through the total gift of self.

Our Lady of Love, giving yourself constantly, pray for us.

7. Prayer for Spouses: see p. 104.

FRIDAY

1. Make the sign of the cross, *slowly, followed by a minute of silence.*

2. Beg for Divine Mercy *while making a profound bow*:

   My God, here we are before you with all our limitations, our sins, our wounds.... (*Make a brief examination of conscience in silence.*) We can do nothing without you, without your infinite mercy, and we humbly ask your forgiveness. We desire with all our strength, with the help of your grace, to follow the path of the Gospel. Have mercy on us, my God.

3. Conjugal chapter (*to be recited by each spouse in turn*):

   N. (*say the spouse's first name*), I ask you to forgive me for the times when I have been inconsiderate and may have hurt you. (*Mention one if appropriate.*)

   I ask God to help me to love you more. Blessed be God for your good qualities. (*Mention one if appropriate.*)

4. Read from the Word of God, *slowly, followed by a short time of silence*:

> Put on then, as God's chosen ones, holy and beloved, compassion, kindness, lowliness, meekness, and patience, forbearing one another and, if one has a complaint against another, forgiving each other; as the Lord has forgiven you, so you also must forgive. And over all these put on love, which binds everything together in perfect harmony. And let the peace of Christ rule in your hearts, to which indeed you were called in the one body. And be thankful. Let the word of Christ dwell in you richly, as you teach and admonish one another in all wisdom, and as you sing psalms and hymns and spiritual songs with thankfulness in your hearts to God. And whatever you do, in word or deed, do everything in the name of the Lord Jesus, giving thanks to God the Father through him. (Col 3:12–17)

5. Recite one Our Father, one Hail Mary, and one Glory Be.

6. Meditation:

> O Mary, here we are in the presence of God, because when two or three are gathered in

the name of Jesus, he is in the midst of us. We believe this because he told us so.

In silence we adore Jesus. We need this heart-to-heart prayer with him in order to persevere in love. Without this attitude of interior listening, our days cannot be organized in an orderly way. With Saint Joan of Arc, let us willingly say, "God is served first", and then all our chores and our concerns will have meaning.

In praying this way, one beside the other in silence, we are united to you, O Mary, who structured your everyday routine on your knees with Joseph, thus choosing the better part. And this enabled you to face the difficulties of life, such as the death of your husband and of your Divine Son.

In the evening of our life, when one of us has returned to the Father, we will appreciate even more the importance of these moments of silent prayer experienced side by side. Indeed, trusting in the Divine Mercy, we will enjoy the renewal of our mutual presence, and our spouse, having become our intimate friend even more by sharing in eternal life, will speak to our heart the language of God.

Saint Joseph, inseparable companion of Mary and patron of the dying, pray that we may always remain together in a state of grace.

Our Lady of Mercy, pray for us.

7. Prayer for Spouses: see p. 104.

SATURDAY

1. Make the sign of the cross, *slowly, followed by a minute of silence.*

2. Beg for Divine Mercy *while making a profound bow*:

   My God, here we are before you with all our limitations, our sins, our wounds.... (*Make a brief examination of conscience in silence.*) We can do nothing without you, without your infinite mercy, and we humbly ask your forgiveness. We desire with all our strength, with the help of your grace, to follow the path of the Gospel. Have mercy on us, my God.

3. Conjugal chapter (*to be recited by each spouse in turn*):

   N. (*say the spouse's first name*), I ask you to forgive me for the times when I have been inconsiderate and may have hurt you. (*Mention one if appropriate.*)

   I ask God to help me to love you more. Blessed be God for your good qualities. (*Mention one if appropriate.*)

4. Read from the Word of God, *slowly, followed by a short time of silence*:

[Address] one another in psalms and hymns and spiritual songs, singing and making melody to the Lord with all your heart, always and for everything giving thanks in the name of our Lord Jesus Christ to God the Father.... Children, obey your parents in the Lord, for this is right. "Honor your father and mother" (this is the first commandment with a promise), "that it may be well with you and that you may live long on the earth." Fathers, do not provoke your children to anger, but bring them up in the discipline and instruction of the Lord....

Put on the whole armor of God, that you may be able to stand against the wiles of the devil. For we are not contending against flesh and blood, but against the principalities, against the powers, against the world rulers of this present darkness, against the spiritual hosts of wickedness in the heavenly places. (Eph 5:19–20; 6:1–4, 11–12)

5. Recite one Our Father, one Hail Mary, and one Glory Be.

6. Meditation:

O Mary, on this day is dedicated to you, we hail you, and we entrust to you in a special way this concern ... (*mention a concern*).

"In the end, my Immaculate Heart will triumph", you said at Fatima. We ask you to give us a childlike heart so as to recognize day by day the signs heralding your triumph. May our everyday preoccupations not conceal what is genuinely at stake in our life. By keeping in our heart and mind the certainty that Jesus is Lord, we guard ourselves from all temptations to despair. Through his Cross, he has reconciled us with himself. May he reconcile us with one another, in our home, our family, with our friends.

Cover us with your mantle, O Mary. Give us holy priests, holy religious, holy families. We pray to you especially for our parish priest, our bishop, and the pope. Strengthen them so that they may always announce the Gospel of salvation.

Blessed Virgin, look also upon those who are not in the flock of the Good Shepherd, the Holy Catholic Church. Grant that they may know him and choose him as the One who has the words of everlasting life.

Finally, obtain for us the strength to witness to the Gospel to the end, to the point of bloodshed, if necessary.

Our Lady, consoling us by the gift of Jesus, pray for us.

7. Prayer for Spouses: see p. 104.

APPENDIX II

Workshop: A Time for Listening

INTRODUCTION

1. This workshop is about taking ten minutes (maximum) to listen *attentively* to one's spouse. The subject should be entirely free, and the spouse listened to must feel completely respected, concerning both the content of his or her proposal and also the need to express it.
2. The good will of both spouses is the meeting point for a greater love.
3. As a moment set aside in conjugal life, this precious time has to be ritualized. In a sense, then, the spouses find themselves as though in a true sanctuary consecrated to conjugal unity. This sense increases through listening to the other.

A few points need to be vigilantly observed:

1. The listening spouse is not allowed to inter-ject to give his or her own opinion or to chal-lenge the other spouse's point, even if he or she feels insulted by the very suggestion. At

that moment, the listener's emotions are his or her own, and the listener must be able to keep them inside.

2. On the other hand, it is recommended that the listener intervene moderately in the conversation to manifest a desire to empathize, to show to the other spouse a willingness to listen with an open mind and heart. In fact, a ten-minute monologue would be difficult for the listener to endure, and the speaker would actually feel alone in his or her expressed desire for renewed communication . . .

3. Here are a few examples of interjections by the listener that could punctuate the ten minutes: "I understand you", "It is true", "That is not easy." Or along the line of simple questions: "What do you mean by that?" or "What is it that makes you say that?"

4. It might be useful for the listener to take notes. Then, at the end, he or she will take about two minutes to reformulate the suggestions of the spouse who was speaking, without judgment or emotion, but calmly and supportively. This important time is the only relatively long moment for the listener to speak. After this, the listening spouse can ask the other whether he or she has correctly reformulated the speaker's

words. Remember that there must be mutual good will; thus the spouse who was speaking will take care not to be too negative in evaluating the efforts of the listening spouse.

5. Another important point: do not start a debate following the reformulation made by the listening spouse.

6. So as not to be disturbed, the couple choose a time and place where no third party will intrude (for instance, a child, family member, friend). The atmosphere immediately preceding the "workshop" must be calm, for it is truly a sacred moment.

7. Eye-contact, facial expressions, gestures, and smiles are essential. External posture reveals the interior attitude.

TOWARD UNION

1. In the final analysis, the objective of the workshop is not only empathy between the spouses but also harmony, so as to achieve a profound union of hearts. Please note that the listener will make an effort not to reply in his own terms to what was expressed, one argument against another, but will seek to share the feelings suggested by the spouse who was speaking, even if the listener is not happy with the grounds of the speaker's reasoning. This is very important.

2. In order to listen to each other better, it is preferable to have only one workshop per day. The listener on one day will be the one listened to the next, and so forth. Each will have his or her turn and his or her day.

3. The rhythm of this alternation can be daily to begin with, then once every two days, then once every three ... To the extent possible, make sure not to leave more than a week between workshops.

4. Recall that on the day when spouses marry in church, they find this time of reciprocal listening at the heart of their exchange of consents. The conjugal "yes" is a harmony of two souls offering themselves, one to the other, unconditionally, with God's blessing. This "yes" is meant to be prolonged every day, explicitly in the workshop of listening and implicitly in the little things of the daily routine. It is the magnanimity of a "yes" that imitates that of Our Lady at the Annunciation. Therefore, it is not a bad thing to invoke Mary, who restores couples each day, so as to choose, with her, to say yes to one's spouse.

PROCEDURE OF THE WORKSHOP

1. In silence, light a candle before an image of the Blessed Virgin Mary.
2. Recite the Prayer to Mary Who Restores Couples (*see below*).
3. The spouse being listened to speaks for a total of ten minutes and is not to be interrupted except for expressions of empathy from the listening spouse.
4. The listening spouse reformulates the substance of what was expressed.
5. After a short moment of silence, recite one Our Father, one Hail Mary, and one Glory Be.

PRAYER TO MARY WHO
RESTORES COUPLES

Mary, we turn to you. Lead us to Jesus,
who has given so much to our household.
We look to your gaze full of goodness,
and we know that under the protection of your
    mantle
there is no anguish that cannot be soothed.
We need so much to be strengthened in our
    good resolutions
and consoled in our trials.
Teach us to become dwelling places
for the infinite love of God
that flows from the Heart of your divine Son,
and also from yours,
to the extent of our good will.
We believe in the Divine Mercy that can forgive
    everything;
teach us to forgive one another.
According to the love that united you to Saint
    Joseph,

give us a heart that is poor and increasingly
    selfless
and open to the interior riches of our spouse.
Tell Jesus for us that we ardently desire to follow
    him
and to love one another more every day.
Mary, you restore couples
by drawing from the grace of the sacrament of
    our marriage.
In your image, may we be renewed by the fire
    of the Holy Spirit.
Mary, restorer of couples, we entrust ourselves
    to you,
so that we may be a living image of the love
that unites Christ to his Church.
With you, we dare believe that from any
    suffering
the luminous joy of Easter morning can shine
    forth.
Amen.